BIBLE STORY CRAFTS
For Little Hands

Ruth Esrig Brinn
illustrated by Sally Springer

KAR-BEN COPIES, INC.
Rockville, MD

BEFORE YOU BEGIN

This book will help you make stories in the Bible come alive!

There are 30 of your favorite Bible stories, each with a picture to color and an easy project to make. Many of the projects are puppets. If you use your imagination you can change the puppet's clothing, and it can become a different character. There are also costumes and instruments you can make so you can become a Bible hero and act out the stories.

The patterns on pages 74-80 are guides to help you make the crafts. Some patterns are shown in several sizes, but you may need to make them even bigger or smaller depending on the size of your finished product. Sometimes you may need to trace only half the pattern.

We've kept the stories short, so if you want to know "what happened next," ask your parents or teachers to tell you!

To Elyasaf Menashe, Bett Aliza, and Col Tmima...
grand additions to the family tree.
—=R.E.B.

Library of Congress Cataloging in Publication Data

Brinn, Ruth Esrig
   Bible Story Crafts for Little Hands / Ruth Esrig Brinn; illustrated by Sally Springer.
   p.   cm.
   ISBN 1-58013-064-x   (pbk.)
   1.Bible Crafts. I. Springer, Sally. II. Title
   BS613.B65 2000   00-022217
   268'.432—dc21

Published by KAR-BEN COPIES, INC., 6800 Tildenwood Lane, Rockville, MD 20852 1-800-4-KARBEN
Printed in the United States of America

CONTENTS

CREATION

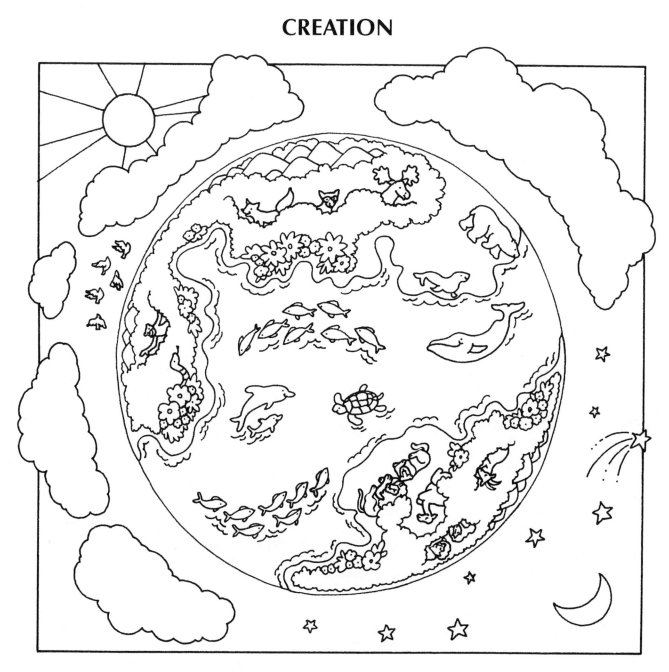

In the beginning, God created heaven and earth.

On the FIRST day, God made light and darkness, morning and evening,

On the SECOND day, the skies and the clouds,

On the THIRD day, sea and land with all kinds of growing plants,

On the FOURTH day, the sun, moon, and stars,

On the FIFTH day, birds in the sky and fish in the sea,

On the SIXTH day, animals and people,

On the SEVENTH day, God finished the work of creation and rested. God blessed the seventh day and called it Shabbat.

CREATION QUILT

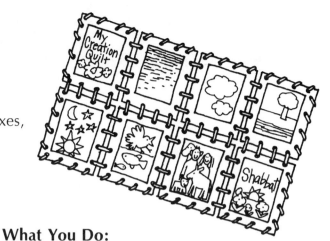

What You Need:

2 pieces white construction paper
4 sheets of cardboard or 2 large empty cereal boxes,
    both the same size
scissors, markers, glue or tape
yarn
hole punch

What You Do:

1. Fold each piece of paper in half and in half again. Cut on the folds. You should have eight rectangles.

2. Write "My Creation Quilt" on one sheet of paper and decorate it. Draw a picture of what happened on each day of creation on each of six other sheets. Write "Shabbat" on the last sheet and draw a Shabbat design.

3. Use the sheets of cardboard, or cut out the front and back panel of each cereal box. Cut each cardboard in half. Glue a picture on each cardboard.

4. Punch evenly-spaced holes around one cardboard. Use this as a guide to mark holes on the other cardboards, and punch out those holes, too.

5. Sew the cardboards together with the yarn, beginning with "My Creation Quilt" and ending with "Shabbat." (If you don't want to use a yarn needle, you can cover the end of the yarn with tape to make it stiff.) Fasten the ends of the yarn to the back with tape.

GARDEN OF EDEN

Adam and Eve lived in the Garden of Eden. They knew they could eat from the fruit of all the trees, except the special tree in the middle of the garden. But the snake persuaded them to taste it. Because they disobeyed, God sent Adam and Eve away from the garden forever.

ADAM AND EVE AND THE SNAKE

What You Need:

White, black, and yellow construction paper
pencil or marker
scissors and glue

What You Do:

1. Fold a sheet of black paper in half. Draw half of a tree shape along the folded edge, and cut it out. Cut out branches along the top. Unfold.

2. Cut another sheet of black paper in half. Fold each piece in two. Draw half of a body shape along the fold of each sheet and cut it out. Unfold.

3. Cut out a long, curvy snake from the yellow paper.

4. Glue the tree and the people to the white paper. Glue the snake onto the tree.

Patterns on pages 74-75

7

NOAH BUILDS AN ARK

The people God created began to do evil. God decided to destroy them. Noah, however, was a good person, so God planned to save him and his family. God told Noah to build an ark with many rooms. Noah did what God told him.

NOAH THE BUILDER

What You Need:

2 short cardboard rolls
colored paper
facial tissue
rubber band
scissors, tape, glue, markers

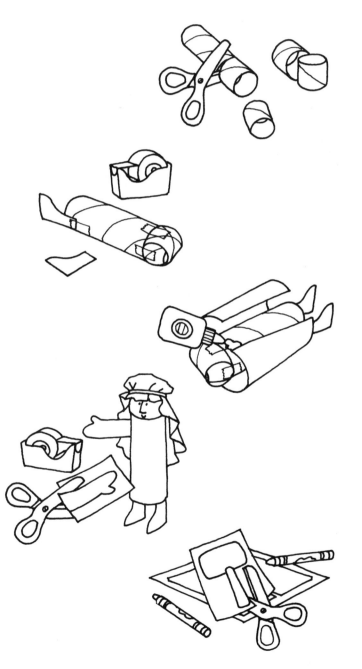

What You Do:

1. Cut two wide strips off of one cardboard roll. Put one inside the other to form a ball. This will be Noah's head.

2. Tape the head to the top of the uncut cardboard roll.

3. Cut two feet from the remaining strip of cardboard. Tape them to the sides of the body.

4. Glue a strip of colored paper around the cardboard roll.

5. Fasten a tissue around the head with a rubber band.

6. Draw and cut out paper arms and tape them on.

7. Draw and cut out paper tools and planks of wood and fasten them to Noah's hands.

Patterns on pages 76-77

9

NOAH'S ARK

Noah and his family moved into the ark. Noah brought pairs of animals into the ark as well. Then it began to rain. It was wet outside, but it was dry and safe inside the ark that Noah had made.

THE ARK

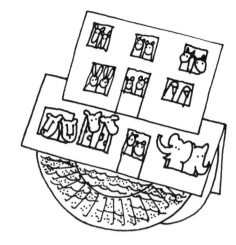

What You Need:

large, white paper plate
2 sheets of colored construction paper
glue, stapler
colored markers

What You Do:

1. Fold the paper plate in half, back sides together. Staple along the fold to reinforce it. The plate should be able to rock back and forth.

2. Fold a sheet of construction paper in half the long way. Draw windows and doors and animals on both sides of the paper. Put glue along the inside edges and glue it over the folded edge of the plate.

3. Fold another sheet of construction paper in half the short way. Draw more windows and animals on both sides of this paper. Put glue along the inside edges and glue it on top of the first strip.

4. Color the bottom of the plate blue to look like water.

THE RAIN STOPS

It rained for 40 days and 40 nights. When the rain finally stopped, Noah sent off a dove to see if the water had dried up. But the dove flew and flew and could not find a place to rest. So the dove returned to the ark. Noah waited a while and sent the dove off again. This time the dove returned with an olive branch in its mouth. Noah waited a while more and sent the dove off a third time. This time the dove did not return. Noah knew that the land had dried up and the people and animals could get off the ark.

THE DOVE AND
THE OLIVE BRANCH

What You Need:

sheet of thin cardboard
sheet of green paper
drinking straw
wire twist
hole punch, tape, markers

What You Do:

1. Draw the shape of a dove on the cardboard and cut it out.

2. Punch a hole for the mouth and put the wire twist through the mouth. Twist to fasten.

3. Cut out small green leaves and tape them to the twist.

4. Tape the straw to the back of the dove.

Pattern on page 78

13

GOD'S PROMISE

God promised Noah to never again send a rain that would flood the world and never again to destroy all living things. As a reminder of that promise God caused a beautiful rainbow to appear in the sky. Today, whenever we see a rainbow, we are reminded of that promise.

THE RAINBOW

What You Need:

white paper plate
sheet of white construction paper
scissors, glue, colored markers

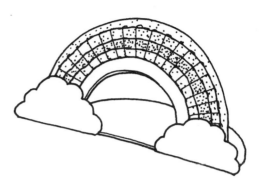

What You Do

1. Fold the paper plate in half with the back sides facing. Unfold it.

2. On one side of the plate draw a half circle. The ends should touch the fold line.

3. Punch a hole inside the half circle with your scissors and cut it out.

4. Color a band of red around the rim at the top. Then add a band of each of the other colors in the rainbow: orange, yellow, green, blue, violet.

5. Cut out some cloud shapes from the white paper. Glue the clouds to the sides of the rainbow.

6. Refold the plate so it stands.

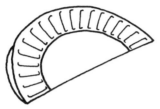

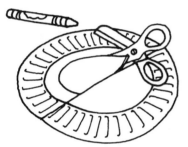

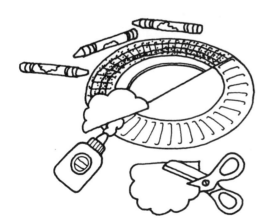

Pattern on page 79

ABRAHAM AND SARAH

God told Abraham and his wife Sarah to leave their home and travel to a land which God would show them. God promised Abraham that he would be the founder of a great nation. His children would be as many as the stars in the sky. Abraham and Sarah traveled to the land of Canaan. They lived in a tent because it was an easy home to move as they traveled.

ABRAHAM AND SARAH'S TENT

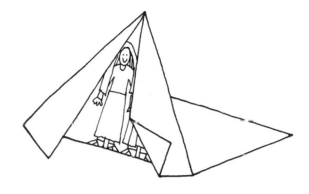

What You Need:

large sheet of construction paper
markers

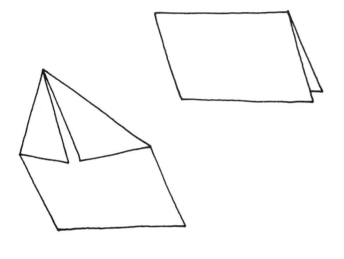

What You Do:

1. Fold the paper in half, short sides together. Unfold the paper.

2. Bring the left corner down along the middle fold until there is a point at the top. Crease the fold. Do the same with the right corner.

3. Fold the bottom half back to make the tent stand.

4. Fold back a small flap on one of the tent openings. Draw a picture of Abraham and Sarah in the tent.

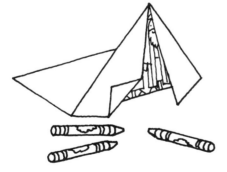

ABRAHAM WELCOMES GUESTS

One day when Abraham was standing outside his tent, he saw three men coming toward him. Abraham welcomed them, invited them to stay and rest, and gave them food and drink and a shady place to sit. The men were really angels and had come with a message from God. They told Abraham and Sarah that they would soon have a baby son. And so it was. They named their baby Isaac.

ABRAHAM
GREETS HIS GUESTS

What You Need:

old sock
plastic sandwich bag
1 cup of rice, or dried peas or beans
2 wire twists
fabric scraps
cardboard
scissors, glue, and markers
decorating scraps (yarn,
    ribbon, paper)

What You Do:

1. Put a cup of rice or beans in the plastic bag and close it tightly with a wire twist.

2. Push it down into the bottom of the sock. Stuff the rest of the sock with fabric scraps and close the sock with a wire twist around the ribbing. Fold the ribbing back over the sock top.

3. Cut out a cardboard circle a little larger than the base of the puppet. Draw toes and sandal straps on it. Glue the puppet onto the circle.

4. Draw a face and put arms on Abraham. Use the decorating scraps to make clothes.

Pattern on page 76

19

FINDING A WIFE FOR ISAAC

Abraham sent his servant Eliezer to find a wife for his son Isaac. On his journey, he saw Rebecca standing at a well. Rebecca welcomed Eliezer and offered him water to drink. She also offered his camels water. Eliezer saw that Rebecca was a kind and caring person. He decided she would make a good wife for Isaac.

20

REBECCA AT THE WELL

What You Need:

sheet of cardboard or large panel cut from a cereal box
2 small brass fasteners
construction paper
scissors, glue, markers

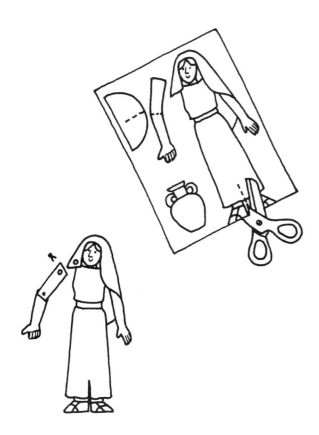

What You Do:

1.   Draw a large outline of Rebecca on the cardboard. Draw only one of her arms. Cut out the shape. Cut a slit at the bottom.

2.   On the leftover cardboard, draw another arm a little longer than the one on the body. Cut it out and cut it in half.

3.   Punch small holes on each half of the longer arm. (See diagram.) Punch a hole near the shoulder of the body. Using the fasteners, link the two parts of the arm and link the arm with the shoulder.

4.   Draw and cut out a water jug and glue it to Rebecca's movable arm.

5.   Cut out a cardboard stand and cut a slit in it. Push the slit on the stand into the slit on Rebecca.

6.   Move Rebecca's arm so she can offer the water to Eliezer.

Patterns on pages 74, 77

REBECCA IS CHOSEN

When Rebecca finished watering the camels, Eliezer gave her a gift of two golden bracelets and a golden ring for her nose! He asked permission of Rebecca's parents to take her back to Canaan to become Isaac's wife.

BRACELETS FOR REBECCA

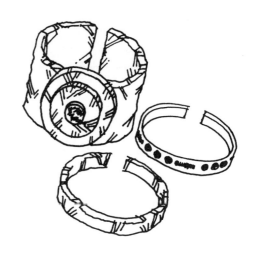

What You Need:

small cardboard roll
sheet of cardboard
silver or gold foil
permanent colored markers
scissors and glue

What You Do:

1. Cut a strip off the roll about three fingers wide. Cut it open. Cover the bracelet with foil.

2. Cut small, medium, and large circles from the sheet of cardboard. Color them with the markers or cover them with foil. Glue them onto the bracelet, one on top of the other.

3. Cut thin strips of cardboard from the roll to make other bracelets. Cover them with foil or color them with markers.

JACOB AND ESAU

Isaac's wife Rebecca gave birth to twins. Esau, the first born, was hairy like an animal. He became a hunter. Jacob, his brother, was a quiet man who stayed near his tent. One day Isaac's sons made a trade. Jacob gave Esau some lentil stew. In exchange Esau told Jacob he could have the right to the special blessing reserved for the first-born son. When Isaac, their father, was very old and nearly blind, he called for Esau to receive his blessing. Jacob covered his smooth arms and hands with animal skins so they would be hairy like Esau's. When Jacob approached his father, Isaac was very confused. The voice sounded like Jacob's, but the hands felt like Esau's. So Isaac was fooled into giving Jacob the special blessing.

A DISGUISE FOR JACOB

What You Need:

shoe
piece of cardboard (or panel of cereal box)
styrofoam tray
colored paper
yarn
scissors, markers, glue

What You Do:

1. Place shoe on cardboard and draw around it. Cut out the shape.

2. Using the leftover cardboard, draw and cut out arms and wide feet. Glue them on.

3. Using the construction paper, draw and cut out another set of arms. Add wide tabs to the sides of each of these arms.

4. Make two slits in the styrofoam tray. Push the feet in the slits to make Jacob stand.

5. Glue pieces of yarn over the paper arms.

6. When you want Jacob to pretend he is Esau, put the hairy arms on top of the cardboard arms and bend over the tabs.

Pattern on page 76

JACOB HAS A DREAM

Jacob left home and set out for his uncle's house. When he became tired, he lay down to sleep out in the open using a rock as a pillow. One night he dreamed of a ladder that stretched from the ground all the way to heaven. Angels were going up and down the ladder. Jacob heard God's voice in the dream. God promised to watch over Jacob and to make him the father of a great nation. When he woke up, Jacob blessed the rock and the place where he had dreamed. He called it Beit El, the House of God.

JACOB'S LADDER

What You Need:

shoebox
construction paper
facial tissue
scissors, markers, glue

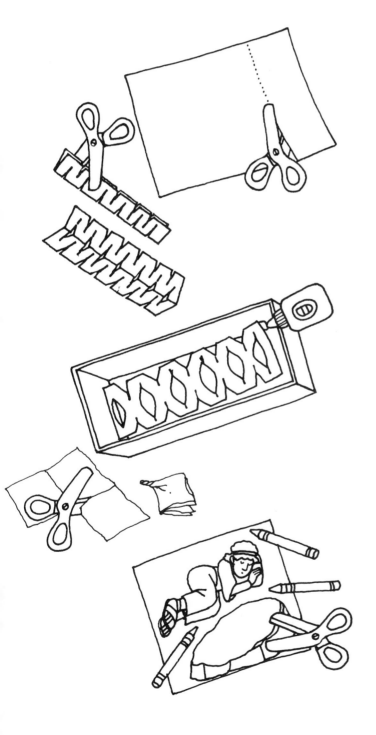

What You Do:

1. Holding the construction paper the wide way, cut a narrow strip off of one side. Fold it in half.

2. Cut a row of deep slits from the folded edge to just before the open edge. Turn the paper around. Between the slits you have made, cut slits from the open edge to just before the folded edge.

3. Carefully unfold the paper and stretch it to make a ladder to fit the box. Glue the ladder ends to the top and bottom of the box.

4. To make the angels, cut a facial tissue into four pieces. Fold each piece in half and in half again. Twist each tissue at the corner fold. Glue the angels to the ladder.

5. With the leftover construction paper, draw and cut out a rock and a figure of Jacob sleeping. Color with the markers. Glue inside the box on the bottom.

Pattern on page 76

JACOB'S WIVES

Jacob arrived at his Uncle Laban's home in Haran. Laban had two daughters. Rachel, the younger daughter, was very beautiful and Jacob loved her very much. Laban told him that he could marry Rachel after he worked for seven years. But when the seven years were over, his uncle tricked him into marrying his older daughter Leah first. Then Jacob had to work another seven years to marry Rachel.

RACHEL AND LEAH

What You Need:

sheet of cardboard or large panel from cereal box
styrofoam tray
scissors and markers

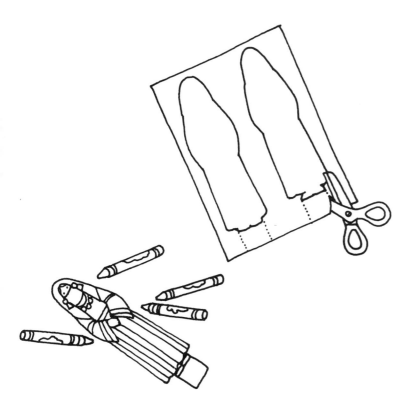

What You Do:

1. Outline the shapes of two women, Rachel and Leah. Draw an extra tab at the bottom of each figure. Cut them out.

2. Draw clothes and jewelry on each woman.

3. Make two slits in the styrofoam tray and put the tabs into the slits so the women can stand.

Pattern on page 74

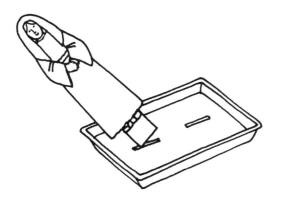

JOSEPH

Jacob had 12 sons. His favorite son was Joseph. Jacob gave him a beautiful coat of many colors. When Joseph's brothers saw that their father loved Joseph more they became angry.

A COAT OF MANY COLORS

What You Need:

sheets of different colored tissue paper
sheet of white construction paper
container of water
paint brush
marker

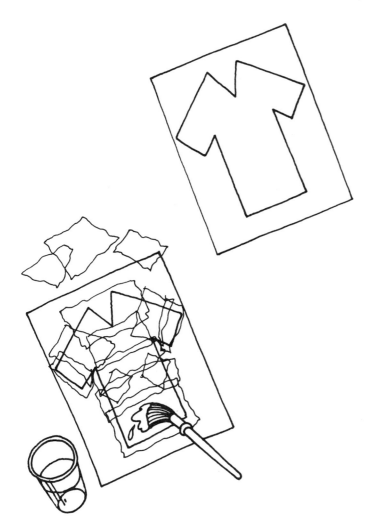

What You Do:

1.   Draw the outline of a large coat on the construction paper.

2.   Tear tissue paper into small scraps. Place them on the coat in a colorful design.

3.   Paint over the tissues with water. The color from the tissues will transfer to the coat. Remove the tissues. There are a few tissue colors that will not transfer. Test each color first on scrap paper.

Pattern on page 80

JOSEPH'S DREAM

One night Joseph dreamed that the sun, the moon, and 11 stars bowed down to him. When he told his brothers about his dream, they became very angry. They assumed the dream meant that Joseph would rule over his family — that his father, mother, and 11 brothers would have to bow down to him.

JOSEPH'S DREAM MOBILE

What You Need:

paper plate
construction paper
stick-on stars
yarn
scissors and marker
glue or tape

What You Do:

1. Draw and cut out the shapes of the sun and moon.

2. Draw and cut out 11 small circles. Put a stick-on star on each circle.

3. Draw and cut out the shape of a larger star. Draw a face on one point of the star.

4. Cut 14 pieces of yarn of different lengths. One should be really long.

5. Fasten one end of the long yarn to the big star and the other end to the center of the plate.

6. Fasten one end of the other pieces of yarn to the sun, moon, and stars, and the other end to the rim of the plate.

7. Fasten a piece of yarn to the back of the plate, so you can hang the mobile.

Pattern on page 79

33

JOSEPH'S BROTHERS TAKE REVENGE

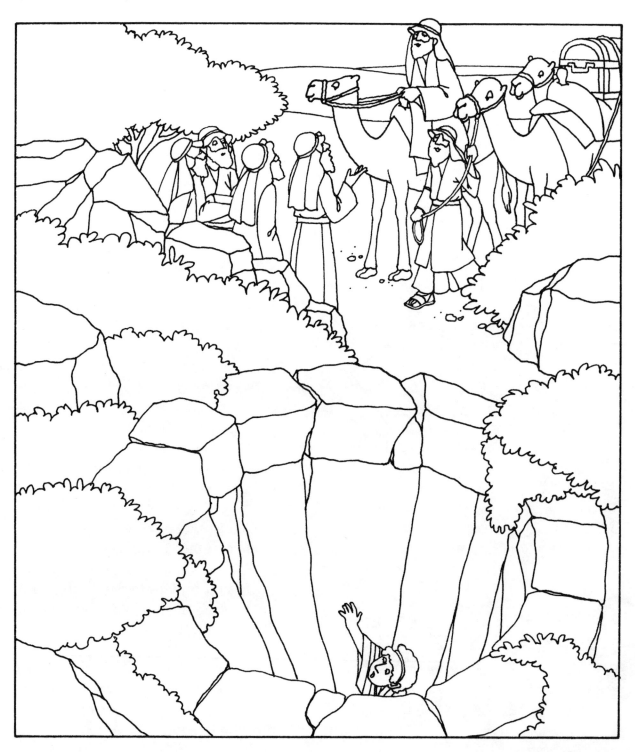

Joseph's brothers were jealous because he was Jacob's favorite son. They were also angry at him because of his dreams. They wanted to do something mean, so they captured him and threw him into a deep, dry well. Traveling merchants pulled Joseph out of the well. They sold him to a caravan of traders on their way to Egypt.

JOSEPH IN THE WELL

What You Need:

construction paper
wire twists
scissors, markers, tape, glue

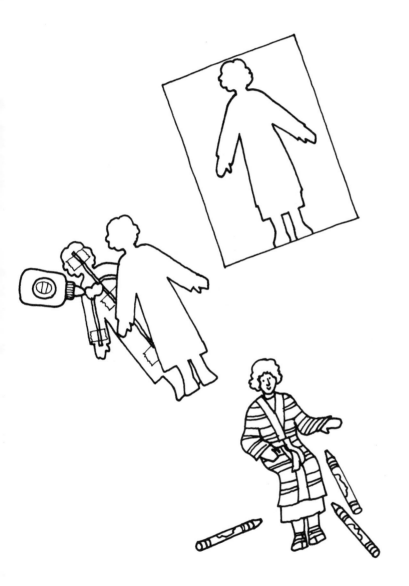

What You Do:

1. Draw a large outline of Joseph on one sheet of construction paper. When you cut it out, put another sheet of construction paper underneath so you cut out two shapes at once.

2. Tape strips of wire twists onto one shape. Glue the two shapes together with the twists inside.

3. Decorate the figure to look like Joseph.

4. The wire twists will help you bend Joseph in many ways.

Pattern on page 74

JOSEPH IN PHARAOH'S COURT

The traders took Joseph down to Egypt and sold him as a slave in Pharaoh's court. Joseph became known as a clever man who could interpret dreams. One night Pharaoh dreamed about a corn stalk that had seven fat ears of corn growing on it. Then seven thin ears of corn began to grow. The thin ears swallowed up the fat ears. Joseph was called on to explain Pharaoh's dream. Joseph said that for the next seven years there would be plenty to eat in Egypt. After that there would be a famine for the next seven years. There would be no food anywhere. He told Pharaoh to collect food during the years of plenty and store it for the years of famine.

PHARAOH'S DREAM

What You Need:

large paper bag
yellow and green tissue paper
scissors, glue or tape

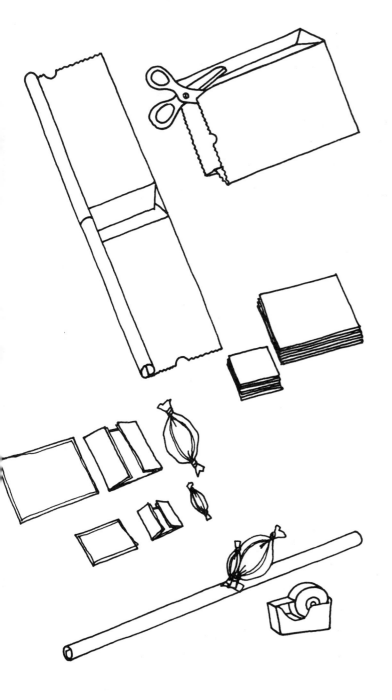

What You Do:

1. Cut along the crease on one side of the paper bag, and cut out the entire bottom. You will have a very large rectangle.

2. With the long side in front of you, roll the paper into a tall corn stalk. Tape closed.

3. Cut the green tissue into seven large and seven small rectangles. Do the same with the yellow tissue.

4. For each ear of corn, put a yellow tissue on top of a green one and fold the sides almost to the middle. Twists the ends together.

5. Make seven fat ears of corn from large rectangles. Fasten them to the stalk.

6. Make seven thin ears of corn from smaller rectangles. Fasten them to the fat ears.

37

JOSEPH'S BROTHERS COME TO EGYPT

Pharaoh appointed Joseph manager over the land. When the famine came, Joseph's brothers came to Egypt to buy food. They didn't recognize Joseph. As they were leaving the palace, the brothers were accused of stealing Joseph's silver cup. Each one was asked to open his grain bag and show what was in it. When Benjamin, the youngest brother, opened his bag, they found the silver cup. It had been put there by a guard. Joseph wanted the brothers to return to the palace so he could reveal himself to his brothers.

JOSEPH'S SILVER CUP

What You Need:

white and black construction paper
foil
cornmeal
scissors, marker, glue

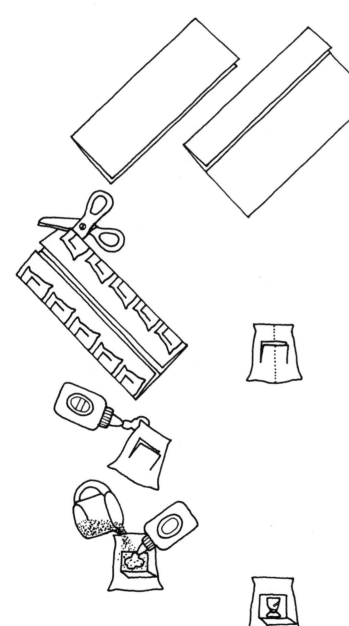

What You Do:

1. Fold a piece of white paper in half. Unfold. Fold each side in to the center fold.

2. On each side, along the folded edge, draw 5 bags. But draw only half the shape. Cut out the shapes.

3. Leaving the bags folded, cut a small slit from the fold to the center, and a small slit down. (See diagram.) Open the bags.

4. On the leftover scrap of paper, draw another bag and cut it out. Fold it in half and cut a small slit from the fold to the center, and a small slit down. This will be Benjamin's bag.

5. Put glue on the outer edges of each bag and paste them onto a dark piece of paper.

6. Put dabs of glue under the openings in the 11 small bags. Sprinkle cornmeal on the glue. Let dry. Shake off what doesn't stick.

7. Shape a tiny cup from silver foil. Glue it in Benjamin's bag.

39

BABY MOSES

A new Pharaoh came to power who did not remember what Joseph did for the Egyptians. He feared that the Jewish people were becoming too numerous and might rise up against him. He ordered that every newborn Jewish baby be thrown into the river. One mother hid her baby in a basket near the edge of the river where the tall grasses grew. The baby's sister, Miriam, kept a watch on him. Pharaoh's daughter, the princess, found the baby and took him out of the basket. She gave him a name, Moses, which means "taken out of the water."

MIRIAM WATCHES HER BROTHER

What You Need:

blue, green, and white construction paper
small paper plate, cut in half
napkin or tissue
wire twist
scissors, tape or glue
colored markers

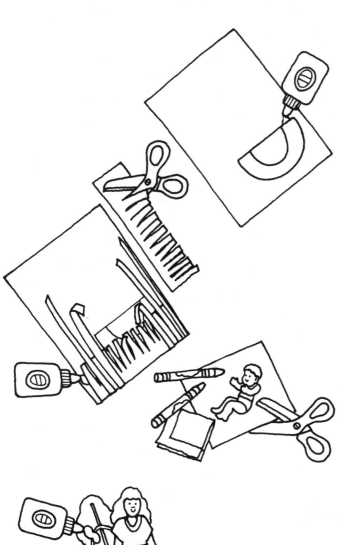

What You Do:

1. Tape or glue the half plate to the bottom of the blue paper. The back side of the plate should be facing you.

2. Cut a long strip from the green paper. Cut many slits to make it look like grass. Paste the strip down covering part of the basket. Cut narrow strips of green paper and paste them down over the grass.

3. Draw and cut out a baby Moses on the white paper. Decorate. Paste Moses in the basket and paste the napkin over him for a blanket.

4. Draw a Miriam shape on a piece of paper. When you cut it out, put another piece of paper underneath so you end up with two shapes. Glue a wire twist on one shape and glue the other shape on top to make a bendable Miriam. Decorate Miriam. Paste her alongside the basket. The wire will enable her to bend to watch over Moses.

Patterns on pages 74, 76

MOSES GROWS UP

Pharaoh made the Jews slaves. His taskmasters treated them very cruelly. One day, Moses saw an Egyptian guard hitting one of the Jewish slaves He struck the guard and killed him. Then Moses fled Egypt. He became a shepherd in a new land. He was kind to his flock of sheep.

TWO OF THE FLOCK

What You Need:

empty cereal box
2 plastic straws
string or yarn
cotton balls
scissors, tape, glue, marker

What You Do:

1. Cut the two wide panels off the cereal box.

2. To make the outline of a lamb, trace your hand on one piece of the cardboard. Spread your fingers, but keep your thumb near your pointer finger. Trace around them. Turn the cardboard around so the fingers are facing down. The fingers are the feet and the thumb is the tail.

3. Draw a connecting line across the top. Draw an oval for the head. Cut out the shape.

4. Glue pieces of cotton onto both sides of the lamb.

5. Make a second lamb the same way.

6. Cut the end of one straw at an angle. Insert it into the other straw. Tape the two straws together.

7. Cut four long pieces of string or yarn. Glue one end of each string to the head and tail of each lamb. Glue the other ends to the straw.

A LAMB WANDERS OFF

One day when Moses was tending his sheep, a lamb wandered off. He followed the lamb into the wilderness.

THE LOST LAMB

What You Need:

short cardboard roll
white tissue paper
white construction paper
pencil
glue, scissors, marker

What You Do:

1. Cut two thin strips off the cardboard roll. Slit each one open. These will be the legs. Fasten each pair to the bottom of the cardboard roll.

2. Using the construction paper, draw and cut out an oval for the head and two small ovals for the ears.

3. Make a slit in the top of the roll. Push the head into it.

4. Fold back the edge on each of the ears and glue to the head.

5. Put glue on a section of the lamb's body.

6. Tear off small squares of tissue paper. Wrap each one around the eraser end of the pencil and stick it onto the glue. Cover the whole body in this way.

MOSES SPIES SOMETHING STRANGE

As Moses followed the lost lamb, he saw the strangest sight. There was a bush on fire, but the bush wasn't burning up. Moses moved closer to get a better look at the burning bush. Suddenly he heard a voice. It was the voice of God.

THE BURNING BUSH

What You Need:

green construction paper
bright yellow or orange tissue paper
toothpick
styrofoam tray
pencil, tape

What You Do:

1. With the pencil, lightly draw a big bush on the green paper, and cut it out.

2. Put the drawing on top of the styrofoam tray, and punch lots of holes all over the bush with the toothpick.

3. Tape the tissue paper to the back of the bush.

4. Tape the bush to a window so you can see the flames shine through the holes.

Pattern on page 75

GOD SPEAKS TO MOSES

Speaking from the Burning Bush, God told Moses to take off his shoes, because he was standing on holy ground. Moses obeyed. God told Moses to return to Egypt and tell Pharaoh to let the Jewish slaves go free. God promised to work miracles to make this happen. So Moses returned to Egypt and gave Pharaoh God's message.

SANDALS FOR MOSES

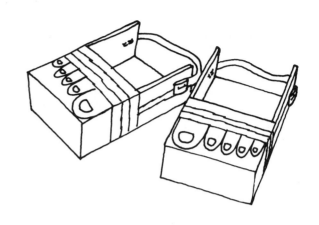

What You Need:

2 small cartons from soy milk
2 thick rubber bands
white paper
scissors, markers, stapler, tape

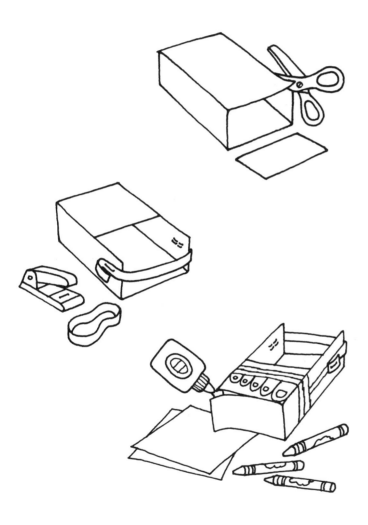

What You Do:

For each sandal:

1. Cut off one end of the carton. Cut enough from the top panel so your foot slides in easily.

2. Cut the rubber band open. Staple the ends to the side panels. Fold over the ends of the rubber band and staple again to make sure they stay.

3. Cover the top and sides with paper. Draw your foot on the top. Draw sandal strips on the top and sides.

THE TEN PLAGUES

Moses asked Pharaoh to let the Jewish slaves go free. When Pharaoh refused, God punished him in many ways. One day when Pharaoh awoke, there were frogs in his bed, frogs on his head, frogs here, there, and everywhere. At first Pharaoh said he would let the people go, but then he changed his mind.

PHARAOH AND THE FROGS

What You Need:

black and white construction paper
green paint or food coloring
paper towel
green and black markers
scissors, glue

What You Do:

1. On the black paper, draw and cut out a shape of Pharaoh in bed. Glue it to the white paper.

2. Pour a little green paint or food coloring on a folded paper towel. It should be moist but not dripping wet.

3. Press your finger or thumb onto the towel and make prints all over the page.

4. Use the green marker to add legs to your frogs, and the black marker to add eyes.

Pattern on page 80

CROSSING THE SEA TO FREEDOM

It took ten plagues before Pharaoh agreed to let the Jewish people leave. Moses led them to the sea. God told him to raise his staff, and when he did, the waters parted, and the people went across on dry land. When they reached the other side, Moses's sister Miriam led the women in singing and dancing as they thanked and praised God for rescuing the Jewish people.

MIRIAM AND HER TAMBOURINE

What You Need:

small cardboad roll
stuffing material
used pantyhose
scraps of fabric and paper
wire twist
scissors, markers, glue

What You Do:

1. Cut several inches off the pantyhose from the toe end. Fill with stuffing to make the head, and fasten with a wire twist.

2. Put glue on the loose ends and push down into the roll.

3. Make slits on both sides of the roll.

4. Cut out two arms and insert them into the slits.

5. Draw and cut out a tambourine and attach it to the arms.

6. Use the fabric and paper scraps to make a head scarf and clothing for Miriam.

Patterns on page 76, 77

AT MT. SINAI

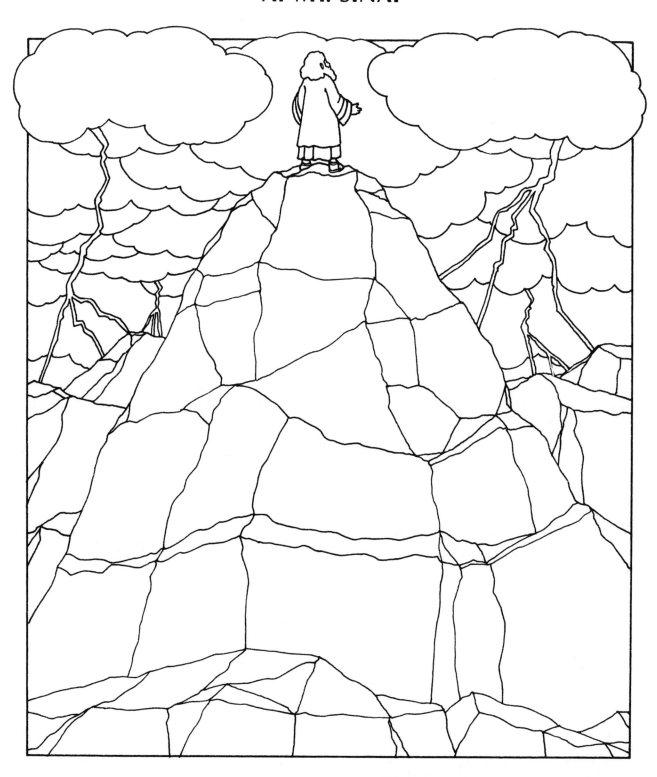

God watched over the Jewish people after they left Egypt. When they came to Mt. Sinai, God told Moses to climb to the top. The people gathered together at the bottom of the mountain to wait for him. There was lightning and thunder all around them.

THE PEOPLE WAIT FOR MOSES

What You Need:

construction paper
scissors, glue, markers

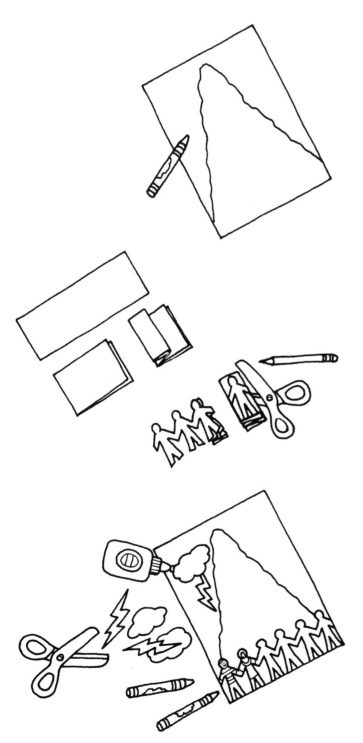

What You Do:

1. Draw a picture of a tall mountain on one piece of construction paper.

2. Cut off a wide strip from another sheet of construction paper. Fold the strip in half, and then again in thirds.

3. Draw the shape of a person. Make the hands reach the fold on each side. Cut out the shape but do not cut the folds. Unfold carefully.

4. Glue the strip of six people to the bottom of the mountain. Decorate them.

5. Draw and cut out clouds and lightning shapes and glue them over the top of the mountain.

THE TEN COMMANDMENTS

After 40 days Moses came down from the mountain. He was holding two tablets with the Ten Commandments written on them. He turned them this way and that way for all the people to see.

MOSES AND THE TEN COMMANDMENTS

What You Need:

old sock
styrofoam cup
long wooden spoon
long strip of polyester stuffing or fabric scrap
construction paper
decorating scraps
wire twist
glue, scissors, markers

What You Do:

1.   To make the head: Glue the end of the stuffing on the spoon. Wrap it around and around until the head is as big as you want it. Stuff it into the toe of the sock. Fasten with wire twist.

2.   Turn the cup upside down. Punch a hole in the bottom large enough for the handle of the spoon. Push the end of the spoon through the opening in the cup.

3.   Stretch the cuff over the bottom of the cup and glue around the rim.

4.   Draw and cut out paper hands and the two tablets, and glue them on.

5.   Use markers and decorating scraps to finish your puppet.

6.   You can move the spoon handle up and down and twist it from side to side so Moses can show the Ten Commandments to all the people.

Patterns on pages 76, 79

RUTH AND NAOMI

Naomi, a Jewish woman, had two sons, both of whom died. She decided to return home to Bethlehem where her family lived. Ruth, one of her daughters-in-law, decided to follow Naomi. She said to Naomi, "Wherever you go, I will go. Your people will be my people. Your God will be my God." When they arrived it was harvest time. In those days farmers left stalks of grain at the edges of their fields for the poor. Ruth went out to a field owned by a man named Boaz to collect some of these stalks so she could bake bread. When Boaz saw how kind Ruth was, he decided to marry her. Ruth and Boaz were the great-grandparents of King David!

RUTH GATHERS WHEAT

What You Need:

styrofoam cup
construction paper
decorating scraps
toothpick
scissors, glue, markers

What You Do:

1. Fold a piece of paper in half. Trace the bottom of the cup. Cut out the two circles you have drawn.

2. Spread glue over one circle. Put the toothpick in the center and cover it with the other circle. Make sure the toothpick sticks out of the circles.

3. Turn the cup upside down. Poke the toothpick through the top of the cup. Put a dab of glue around the hole to keep it tight.

4. Draw and cut out arms and fasten them to the sides of the cup.

5. Draw and cut out a bundle of grain and glue it onto the hands.

6. Use markers and decorating scraps for Ruth's face and clothing.

Patterns on pages 75, 76

DAVID AND GOLIATH

Goliath was a mighty giant in an army fighting the Jewish people. He dared anyone to fight him alone. None of the Jewish soldiers was willing to take a chance against so mighty a man. David, a shepherd boy, was too young to serve in the army. But with stones from his slingshot he had killed a bear and a lion when the animals had attacked his flock. And he was determined to kill that mighty giant Goliath. Goliath laughed when David presented himself. But David took a smooth stone he had found in the brook, placed it in his slingshot, and hit Goliath right in the middle of the forehead. King Saul and the people praised David for his courage.

DAVID IS READY TO FIGHT

What You Need:

small cardboard roll
used envelope
facial tissue
construction paper
string or thread
scissors, marker, glue

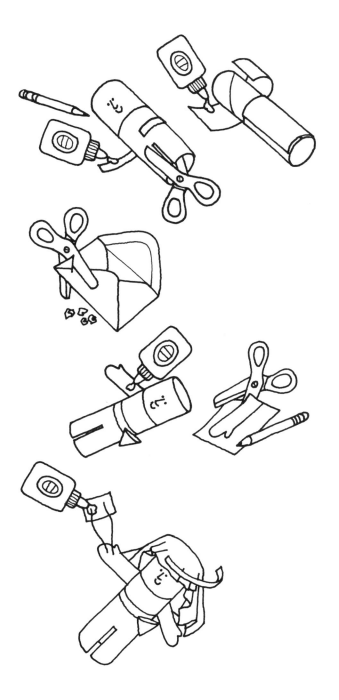

What You Do:

1. Cover the top third of the roll with white paper. Cover the rest of the roll with paper of another color. Draw a face on the white part, and cut out openings for legs on the colored part. Cut a thin strip of paper and glue it around for a belt.

2. Cut off a corner off the envelope and fasten it to the belt. Crush tiny pieces of paper to make stones and put them in the envelope.

3. Draw and cut out arms and glue them at the sides.

4. Cut out a small rectangle for the sling. Cut two short pieces of thread. Glue one end of each piece of string to each end of the slingshot. Glue the other ends to David's hand.

5. Fold the tissue and arrange it as a headcovering. Cut a thin strip of paper and fasten it around the head covering.

Pattern on page 76

JONAH

God asked Jonah to go to Nineveh and tell the people there to stop their evil ways. Jonah did not want to go. Instead he boarded a boat and sailed to a faraway land. When a bad storm came, the other sailors blamed it on Jonah. They tossed him overboard. Jonah was swallowed by a whale. Jonah prayed to God. The whale spit him out onto dry land and he was saved. Then Jonah agreed to take God's message to the people of Nineveh.

JONAH IN THE WHALE

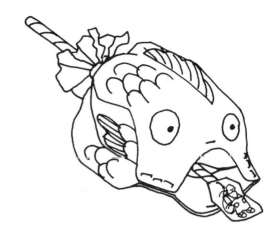

What You Need:

small paper bag
2 plastic straws
3 paper napkins
wire twist
construction paper
markers or paint
stapler, scissors, tape

What You Do:

1. Staple the bottom corners of the bag together to form a mouth. Cut a slit in the middle of the mouth. Staple the sides together to keep the mouth open.

2. Cut one straw end at an angle and insert it into the other straw. Tape the straws together where they join.

3. Draw and cut out a small picture of Jonah. Staple it onto one end of the straw. Put the straw into the bag. The end with Jonah on it should be near the mouth.

4. Crush the napkins into balls and stuff them inside the bag.

5. Close the bag around the straw and secure with wire twists.

6. With paint or markers, color the whale and draw eyes, mouth, flippers, and tail.

7. Watch Jonah go in and out of the whale's mouth as you move the straw.

Pattern on page 76

On the following pages there are costumes and musical instruments you can make so that you can dress up as characters from the Bible and act out their stories.

WEARABLE TUNIC I

What You Need:

old pillow case
old necktie or piece of rope
scissors

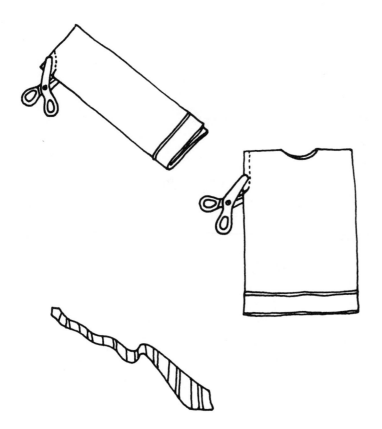

What You Do:

1. Fold the pillowcase in half, long ends together. Cut an opening between the two folded edges. It should be large enough to fit over your head easily.

2. Open the pillowcase. Cut openings for arms along the sides.

3. Use the necktie or rope as a belt.

WEARABLE TUNIC II

What You Need:

2 towels
rope or old necktie
scissors, masking tape

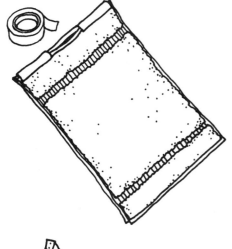

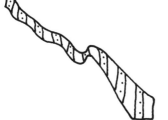

What You Do:

1. Put the towels together. Tape the top edges on each side, leaving the center open for your head.

2. For added strength, open the towels and put extra tape on the inside.

3. Use the necktie or rope as a belt.

BEARD

What You Need:

used pantyhose
white or gray yarn
scissors

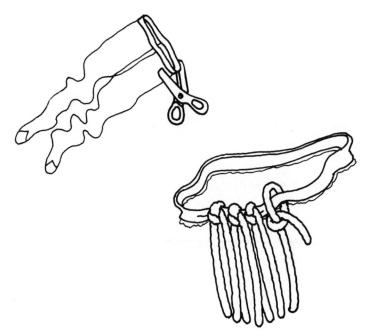

What You Do:

1. Cut off the waistband from the pantyhose. It should fit around your head and under your chin.

2. Cut pieces of yarn twice as long as you want the beard to be. Tie each piece of yarn onto the band. Fill up the bottom half of the band.

HEADCOVERING

What You Need:

hand towel
used pantyhose
scissors

What You Do:

1. Cut the band off the pantyhose.

2. Put the towel on your head.

3. Stretch the band over the towel.

SHEPHERD'S STAFF

What You Need:

three long cardboard rolls
two large paper bags
scissors, glue

What You Do:

1. Twist and push the ends of the cardboard rolls together to make one very long roll.

2. Cut out the side panels from the paper bags, and put aside to use for another project. Do not cut the bottoms of the bags.

2. Open the bags so you have two very long strips of brown paper.

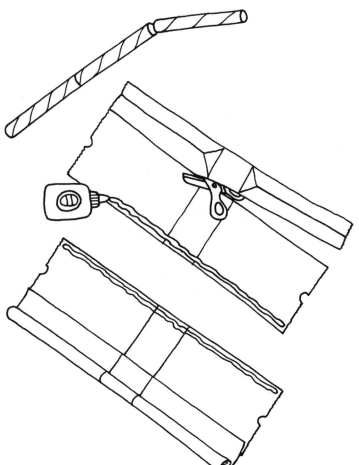

3. Put glue along the long edge of each strip.

4. Place the long cardboard roll on top of one glued end Roll it around and around. Continue rolling onto second paper strip, but this time begin with the dry end and roll around to the glued edge. Seal tightly.

ARMLET

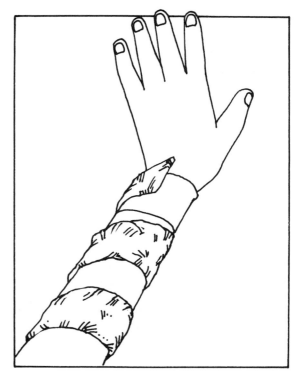

What You Need:

long paper roll
aluminum foil
paint and paint brush
scissors and glue

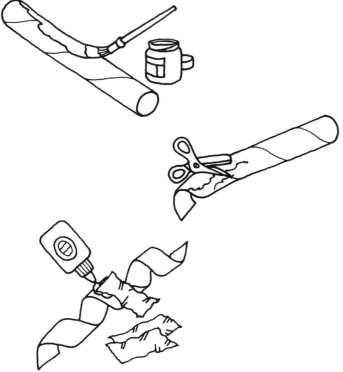

What You Do:

1. Paint the roll.

2. Cut along the spiral markings to open the roll.

3. Glue bands of foil to decorate.

BRACELET

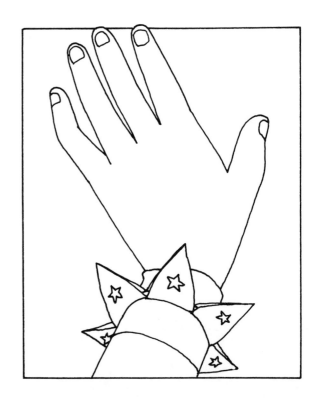

What You Need:

rubber band that fits loosely over your wrist
colored paper
stick-on stars
scissors and glue

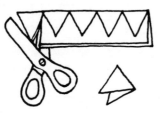

What You Do:

1.   Cut off a long strip of colored paper. Fold in half, long edges together.

2.   Draw triangles along the folded edge and cut them out. Do not cut the folded edge.

3.   Glue the triangles around the rubber band and decorate with stars.

TAMBOURINE

What You Need:

2 paper plates
hole punch
wire twists
buttons, or pull tabs from cans

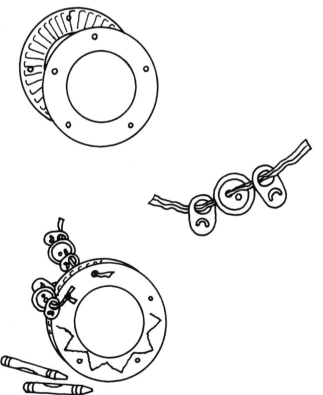

What You Do:

1. Put plates together front sides facing. Punch four or five holes evenly around the rims.

2. String some buttons or pull tabs on each wire. Push the wire through each set of holes and twist the ends together.

3. Decorate the plate if you wish.

DAVID'S HARP

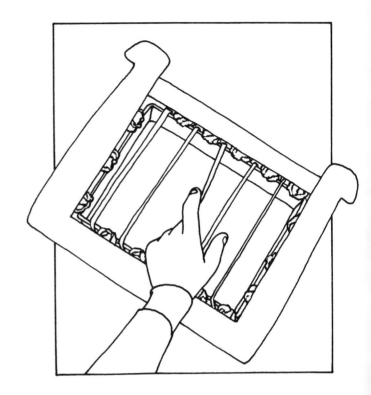

What You Need:

styrofoam tray
rubber bands of various sizes
constructon paper
tissue paper
glue, scissors, marker

What You Do:

1. Stretch five rubber bands across the tray. Try different sizes until you get sounds you like.

2. Crush pieces of tissue paper into small balls. Glue them around the top rim of the tray.

3. Cut a strip of construction paper and glue it onto the balls across one long side of the tray. The balls will keep the paper from touching the rubber bands.

4. On the construction paper, draw and cut out a three-sided harp design and glue it onto the balls around the tray.

5. Glue the ends of the harp design to the ends of the paper strip.

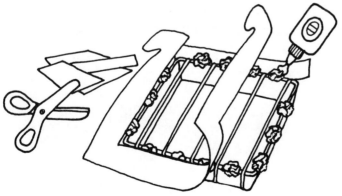

Pattern on page 77

SHEPHERD'S FLUTE

What You Need:

4 plastic straws
yarn
construction paper
scissors, tape, glue

What You Do:

1.   Cut the three straws into different lengths. Do not cut the fourth straw.

2.   Lay a piece of tape, sticky side up on the table.   Place the seven straw pieces according to length side by side on the tape. The top edges should be even.

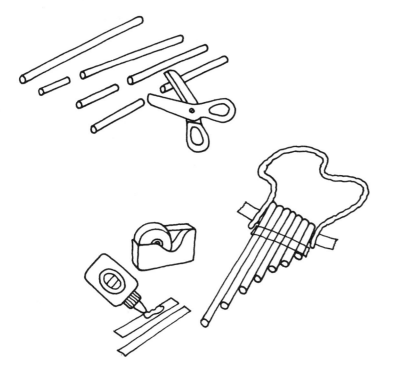

3.   Cut a piece of yarn long enough to slip over your head easily. Place the ends of the yarn on the tape on either side of the straws.   Fold the tape over to secure the yarn and straws.

4.   Cut another piece of tape and put it across all the straws down toward the middle.

5.   Glue thin strips of construction paper on top of the tape.

6.   You can wear the instrument around your neck. To play, blow gently across the tops of the straws.

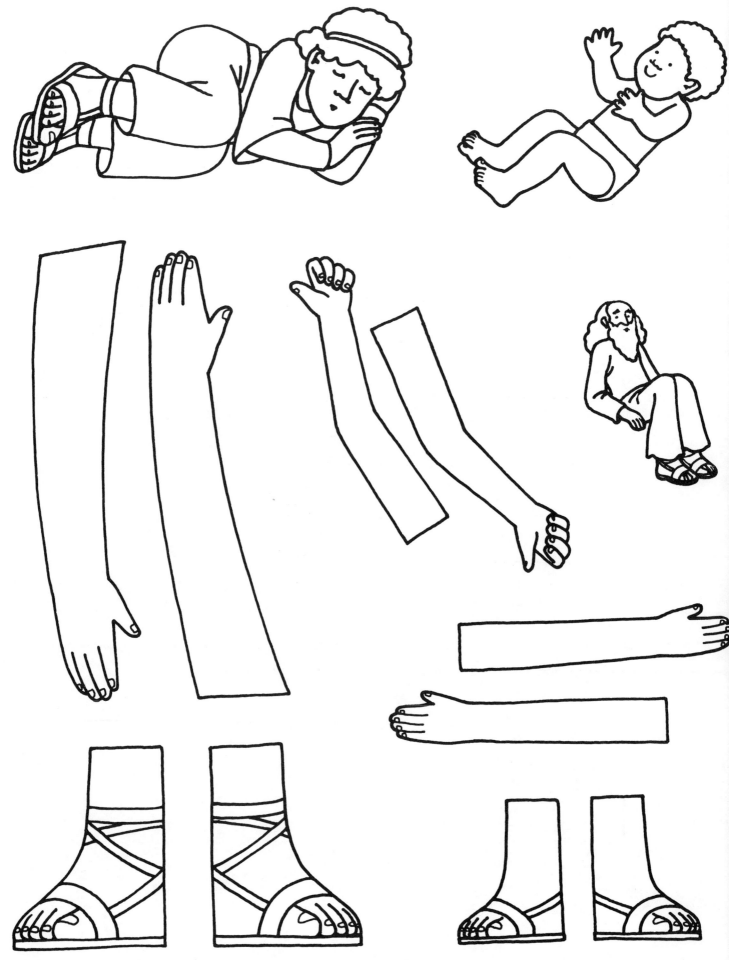